PRACTICAL ADVICE

FOR

WHOLESOME LIVING

PRACTICAL ADVICE
FOR
WHOLESOME LIVING

Charles Arthur Shipp, Sr.

iUniverse, Inc.
New York   Bloomington

Practical Advice for Wholesome Living

iUniverse books may be ordered through booksellers or by contacting:

iUniverse
1663 Liberty Drive
Bloomington, IN 47403
www.iuniverse.com
1-800-Authors (1-800-288-4677)

ISBN: 978-1-4502-4808-2 (pbk)
ISBN: 978-1-4502-4809-9 (ebk)

Printed in the United States of America

iUniverse rev. date: 9/3/2010

Contents

Preface

The world we live in may not be as complicated as some will have you believe; however, I will acknowledge that we've had some difficult days with the war in Afghanistan, crime in our cities, and declining respect for one another, to name a few horrendous situations that have invaded our communities and altered our lifestyles. Even with the many disappointments, we have learned to lean on those who have remained strong and faithful, and who have offered words of comfort, encouragement, and support in times of need.

Practical Advice for Wholesome Living is a collection of experiences that I have compiled over the years. They have assisted me in providing instructions to a captious group of students and staff during my tenure as an administrator in public and private schools.

The primary reason for presenting these ideas is to invite the reader to concentrate on phrases that will promote hope, faith, and encouragement for those who are looking for a better lifestyle. Each notion is meant to inspire, be thought provoking, and serve as sermon topics for ministers of the gospel.

Acknowledgments

I would like to thank God for granting me the experiences that motivated me to write this book.

To my colleagues, past and present: I am profoundly grateful for your encouragement and prayers during my sojourn with this project.

SECTION 1:
ADVICE TO ENCOURAGE

A smile is greater than a frown, and eventually, a smile will defeat a frown.

If you can't be the first one in the integrity line, at least be in line because obtaining integrity will get you ahead.

Others won't value you if you don't value yourself.

When you discover that you are the last person running in a race, you can do one of two things: quit, or run faster.

Be careful who you tell your problems to because everybody can't be good at problem solving.

If you stumble, try not to fall. If you fall, try to land on your back, so you will know from whence you came.

The Boy Scout motto is perfect for Christians: "Be Prepared." We should always have our armor on when facing day-to-day situations.

It is never too late to grow up. Every day that you live should be a day in which you gain maturity.

You never fail unless you fail to make every effort to do your best.

In order to avoid family conflict, learn how to turn *to* one another, as opposed to turning *against* one another.

Don't fret while doing your best; you are not going to please everyone.

Don't sit around in self pity; develop strength in your time of weakness by encouraging yourself.

If you lose the key to the door of forgiveness, don't worry; God can provide you with a duplicate.

Your internal thinking will affect your external disposition, so think positively.

If you can't say anything positive while talking to someone, practice listening instead of speaking.

Never complain about the decisions made by others unless you have a solution.

You should be the first one to find the solution, especially when you are the cause of the problem.

In order to keep peace with others, don't allow your mind to manufacture trouble.

Don't hesitate to put into practice the solution to your dilemma once it has been established.

When you find yourself falling apart, use the GLUE (God's Love Unites Everyone) that is always available.

God has graced us with special gifts or talents; it is up to us to make them work.

Don't let the time clock of life run out on you before

you take your best shot; you may not get another opportunity to participate in the game called life.

Don't be afraid to approach your enemies, because you can't conquer what you are not willing to confront.

Nobody feels good about feeling bad!

A good finish demands a strong start.

In order to obtain a meaningful education, one must be a willing participant in learning, directed by teachers who love the profession, and encouraged by those who love you.

Just because you are the guy who is always chosen last on a team doesn't mean you are not as good as everyone else.

Forget about your failures and concentrate on the many possibilities that await you.

You need to keep your options open, because without them there are no choices.

When you go through a desert experience, don't allow the mirage of life to cause you to turn back.

Don't destroy the bridge you have crossed many times by not forgiving those who have wronged you, because you may have to cross it one more time.

Ask the Lord for guidance in the form of prayer when

you are making difficult decisions, and the margin of errors will be profoundly lessened.

Be realistic; you can determine without being coached whether you are headed toward destruction.

You don't have to be a baseball player to step up to the plate and admit your mistakes.

In order to love everybody, you first must love yourself.

It is not only essential to focus on the principle of all matters, but it is as important to maintain a high interest level as well.

Don't drown in the past by reliving old problems.

Always muscle enough strength to encourage yourself.

Practice being an upbeat person even in a world of confusion; it is therapy for the soul.

Change is a process; it is a continuation of the passion to do the right thing.

Think positively and it will yield positive results.

True love is the sharing of everything, including the good, the bad, and the ugly.

Don't quit on yourself when things are not going the way you desire; keep in mind that God has not given up on you.

Don't count yourself out or put yourself down. There are a lot of people doing that for you, so keep your chin up.

"Right" will always be your greatest legal defense and will give you with the best opportunity to be vindicated.

Never give in or give up; when you think you're down to nothing, God will give you the strength to endure.

Never turn away from those who are trying to turn you around.

It is not good enough for us to just exist on earth; we must press to become productive in our lives and in the lives of others.

Let go of your pride and hold on to dignity.

Learn not to hate your troubles but learn from them so as not to repeat them.

Continue to be true to yourself, for there are those who look up to you and believe in you.

Although the torch of courage may be flickering, and you can hardly see your way, keep pressing onward. Tomorrow will be a brighter day. Courage is something you must have from the beginning.

When you are misunderstood by some, don't neglect to understand that, if in all honesty and sincerity you have given your best; be proud of your efforts no matter what.

Don't become mentally lazy; refrain from responding "I don't know" to a simple question.

Don't permit your attitude to get in the way of your aptitude; don't let it keep you from reaching your altitude in life.

When you have the opportunity to choose an instrument from the "tool box" of essentials, let me suggest that you select the tool called "love," for love is the ultimate tool and never fails.

An achiever is someone who not only takes advantage of the many opportunities afforded him but has the yearning to excel at everything he does.

It doesn't matter how ambitious you have become, it will not profit you to end up as nobody.

Everybody is somebody's somebody.

When you defeat yourself, there is no need to develop strategies; however, if you are going to overcome those problems that are trying to defeat you, it is imperative to develop strategies that will work on your behalf.

Do all you can to keep good health, and don't rely on others to keep it for you!

You are never forced to follow to follow Jesus; He extends the invitation to everyone.

If things are not going the way you would like, try something different and see if the results work in your favor.

With a closed hand, you will be unable to receive or give a blessing.

You can obtain perfect peace by believing that no matter what others think of you, you have done your best.

Put a little laughter in your life and it will eventually improve your disposition.

Laughter is the flame that keeps our hearts radiantly aglow.

We should give God all the credit for the things we possess.

Take a little time to thank God daily for all you are experiencing; it could be much worse, so count your many blessings while you are able.

Our divine Savior said, "We are to love our neighbor as ourselves," but unfortunately, many have failed to listen.

Don't start blaming God for what you don't have; instead, blame yourself for what you have not asked for. We have not received because we have not asked.

Don't invest in things that will not produce dividends; don't bank on people you can't trust.

You never get too old to improve those things you are deficient in.

Although you can't literally fix your eyes on God, He is much closer than you know.

The present is now, so living in the past denies us what is to be.

Life is livable, mountains are climbable, rivers are crossable, and people are more lovable when you hold on to God's unchanging hand.

You might not have been as successful as you once thought you would be, but if you keep on believing, God can make your dreams come true.

Challenges are good for the soul; they bring the best out of us by allowing us to perform at the highest level of our competency. Never turn down a good challenge.

When you want to perform at your best, stay focused and don't let small or large issues get you off track. No one knows your strengths or weaknesses better than you.

A true man is one who is guided by the spiritual foundation he has built within his home, church, and community. Additionally, he does not allow difficult circumstances to prohibit him from making the right choices.

Strive to be rock-solid in all that you say and do, and great returns will come back to you.

Not many people are where they should or want to be, but at least they are not where they once were. Because of some good people who have made their way into their life, they have become better people.

Making an impact on others should be one of our goals; however, impacts come in two forms: good and bad. We want to have a positive impact on youths so that others will see productive growth by how they conduct themselves.

Rather than playing the Lone Ranger, find a friend who has unquenchable love that will not diminish by adversity.

Strive to be the best individual you possibly can be, even though you may stumble and fall at times. A righteous person, with God's help, will recover, but the evil person faces permanent destruction.

You know you have made a positive impact on your performance when the results are in your favor.

Don't let your past catch up with you. In case it does, start doing those things that will not make you feel shame.

God created you and made you special; therefore, you don't have to change anything that He has done, but you may want to change the way you act.

An average swimmer may not be able to reach one end of the pool to the other with just one long stroke; therefore, it is important for the swimmer to use all the skills necessary to be successful.

It is impossible to separate yourself from your words, so make your words bond with your common sense.

Be dependable by keeping your promises intact; after all, promises are made to not be broken.

It is a good practice to be attentive to advice given you, but it is also advisable to have an opinion of your own. Learn to think for yourself.

Everyone who obeys the law should not have reason to feel guilty.

It should not be difficult for an honest person to say goodbye to evil.

There are few benefits without risk, and there are few risks worth taking for you not to be benefited.

One of the greatest gifts given is the gift of good health, and we should demonstrate our appreciation by taking good care of ourselves.

It doesn't matter how low you have fallen, you can still

be elevated to the highest level if your determination is compatible with a positive attitude.

To close the mouths of those who tell you you're wrong, do what's right.

When life deals you a bad hand, you can either throw it in or play with what you have been given.

Your character, your friendship, your home, or your life cannot survive without a firm foundation. Construct a good base, and what is built on it will last a lifetime.

There is a call for those with integrity to step forward and join in partnership with common sense to help raise the awareness of peace and love in communities everywhere.

To overcome barriers that confront us, we can defeat those barriers by asserting the willpower commonly known as determination.

Periodically, conduct a self-examination to ascertain whether you are meeting the standards you have set for yourself.

Your endurance can be self-tested by hanging in when things are at their worst.

It is an indictment of oneself when you fail to recognize your potential, but it is more disgraceful to have potential and fail to put it into practice.

"Do unto others what you would have them do to you" is a magnificent way to keep the peace.

Learn how to stand up for yourself; there will be people trying to put you down.

You can't move forward until you stop moving backward; walking backward will only allow you to see where you've been, not where you're going.

Leave your troubles behind, and stop carrying them around. Can't you see their weight and stress are slowing you down?

Life is not to be taken for granted; it is our responsibility to make the necessary adjustments on a daily basis to improve ourselves.

Don't let your condition be your conclusion.

SECTION 2:
ADVICE FOR WISDOM

As a prospector searches for gold, one must search for wisdom.

Let your haters become your motivators.

If you flirt with Satan, you will become a prostitute to sin.

It is foolish to wear a short skirt and spend the entire day pulling it down.

Straddling the fence is like being on a stationary bike—you don't move forward or backward.

One way to avoid an argument with others is to hold conversations with yourself.

Don't let a fool give you advice unless you are willing to accept a foolish response.

Don't get so low whereby you aren't able to raise your pride to admit when you have made a mistake.

It is better late than never, unless you end up at a place where you shouldn't have been in the first place.

You are blessed to know that you know when you are able to perform a task with little or no effort.

Don't start swimming until you hit water.

Don't let the statement "I don't know" be the end result. Press to find an answer.

A wise person is one who knows when not to speak.

Don't do to yourself what your haters are trying to do to you. If you work hard at being down on yourself, you make the life of your enemies too easy.

If you have a habit of talking to yourself, make sure you are alone.

Occasionally, it's good to be tough; however, it is usually better to try a little tenderness.

Don't waste your time arguing with a fool, for he has nothing to lose.

Who you pretend to be is not what others see; then again, who are you really trying to please—others, or yourself?

Don't change your mind unless you are willing to changes your attitude.

Making a decision while angry is really not your decision but that of the devil.

When working in a hostile environment, if you want respect, take it to work with you.

Changing your mind is the first step toward changing your life.

Don't let what you believe people are thinking persuade you, unless you are capable of reading minds.

Are you the type of person who gets upset when your pet parakeet calls you stupid?

It is practical to make change with money, but don't let money change you.

Be realistic. Carrying an umbrella around will not make it rain; however, having an umbrella while it's raining will not make it stop.

Be careful what you say because your thoughts will eventually become your destiny.

It is bad enough when you tell lies about others, but when you lie about yourself you have gone too far.

It is good to build a house, but you have to build a relationship before it becomes a home.

Acting insane is dangerous, especially in a park where squirrels love to gather nuts.

The first impression is not always correct.

If you don't want to be the tail, stop lagging behind.

Don't waste time on things you can't do anything about.

It is difficult to make demands if you are not in demand.

Hard times don't change the truth, but the truth can change hard times.

You can't put your foot in your mouth if you learn to keep it planted on a firm foundation.

A bird in the hand could get you awfully dirty.

A hint to the wise is sufficient enough only when the hint is taken seriously.

It's not always about the "how," but more importantly about the "who."

Don't pretend you know everything unless you were created immediately after the world was formed.

If you have to call a timeout during a basketball game to discover who you are playing, it may be too late to develop strategies for a victory.

A wise person may say, "You can ask me anything; however, you may not appreciate my answer."

Sometimes it is best to be satisfied with what you have than to obtain what you don't want.

Which is worse: living with someone you can't remember, or living with someone you're trying to forget?

In order to get a different result, you have to do something different.

Don't think swimming in the rain will make the water wetter.

Joining the bike club without owning a bike

is like trying to operate a lawn service without lawnmowers.

Using dice without numbers is not only a disadvantage, it is useless.

The person who takes care of what has been provided him is a good example of practicing stewardship.

You don't have to carry around razorblades in order to prove you are a sharp thinker.

If the light at the end of the tunnel is a train, you are on the wrong track.

Wisdom is knowing what to do when you are under pressure.

When caught in a lie, you become the personification of helplessness.

A person who is caught up in egocentric endeavors will become unfocused and eventually drift into foolishness.

A selfish person is defined as a "mefirster": myself always, and "I" only.

Kindness and good fortune will not continue to flow to you unless they flow from you.

To obtain strength in yourself, break the habit of worrying.

If you feed your body and not your mind, you soon will be top light and bottom heavy.

If your intention is to do the right thing, God will transmit the right opportunities to you.

Think before you speak and never force a response without substance.

You are not an airplane pilot, so stop trying to navigate others' destinies.

Stop being so critical of others and start looking for something to praise others for.

Don't be good at being bad; it is not intended to be a profession.

No man can change himself without help from God.

Negative thinkers are negative doers.

Using proper English while communicating is important; it is equally important to exercise common sense while speaking.

Criticism absent of counseling is ineffective.

It doesn't matter how tall you are, life is still considered short.

Having self-confidence will improve your disposition far better than being self-centered.

You become a student of your enemies when you learn how to treat others badly.

There is no right way to do wrong.

Sometimes it is not what you are holding but what you let go of that is important.

Don't make foolish rules, because eventually you will be the one having to live by them.

Spend your time wisely; only a fool thinks he will live forever.

Don't expect to plant a particular seed and obtain a different harvest.

Be careful what comes out of your mouth; your tongue can be so sharp that it will cut your own throat.

Sometimes you have to take a short loss for a long-term gain.

Opportunity always comes disguised as work.

People who fail to love others have the greatest limitations.

If you fail to plan, your plans will surely fail.

A pity party only invites those who have no ambition.

Living without being loved is synonymous to clipping a bird's wings and prohibiting it from flying.

A visionary is a person who establishes his end before he starts.

In order to be the master of your mind, learn how to think for yourself.

Having what you need to succeed but failing to put it into action is just as bad as not having it in the first place.

Cultivate your imagination by putting yourself in the place of others.

Don't make a habit of telling a half truth; it will save you time trying to explain the other half later on.

Don't wait until you experience pain to cry out for help; always let your feelings be known.

A fool who knows that he is a fool may not be so foolish after all.

If you insist on being a foolish person, then be foolish for the right reasons.

An April fool is just as bad as being a fool in any other month of the year.

Make no mistake about it: there is nothing so unfitting as a fool in luxury and a slave in power.

Words of encouragement are not like timeouts in a basketball game; you should not be forced to use them.

Laughter is the cosmetic surgeon that eliminates the unaesthetic appearance.

There is no substitute for honesty.

Don't walk around with a long face just because you think you have gotten the short end of the stick.

You don't need a measuring stick to measure up to your responsibilities.

Pierced ears leave a hole for earrings, but a look can be so piercing it can leave a hole in your heart.

If you keep taking steps backward, you will never reach your destination.

It takes more energy, more muscles, and more time to be arrogant than it does to be gracious and humble.

If you aren't willing to bring along your A game when you compete, you will end up letting your opponent watch you defeat yourself.

Nothing is discovered without an expedition.

Whether you are wise or unwise, it really doesn't matter in the grave. The wise and unwise persons will be equally dead; therefore, it doesn't pay to boast about what you have in terms of materialistic value, but rather where your soul will spend eternity.

Spend time making your life meaningful. There is a

time for everything, but the most important thing to remember is that time is too valuable to waste.

You don't have to be an engineer to build a good relationship, but it helps if you had experience as a firefighter, because in order to maintain a good relationship, you have to be able to put out fires.

It is no secret that some bad people can make you good.

Common sense is no longer common.

Always invite your conscience in on your conversations with others. If you are confronted with a difficult question, let your conscience be your guide.

Don't exceed your means; it could very well be your end.

It is an abomination to have your lips come unglued with falsehoods; the words from your lips should be your bond.

When you are doing your best to impress others but excluding yourself from this process, you are admitting that you are less worthy than your circle of friends.

We should practice discretion inwardly, because it is more important than outward beauty.

A wise man will get advice from a prudent person before drawing a conclusion. The results of our ghostly decisions will haunt us for the rest of our life, so make the best decision with sound judgment.

Self-serving is only beneficial during periods of isolation.

Don't settle for mediocrity but forever venture to be the best at whatever you do.

Always be yourself, and don't let others change you without your permission.

If the truth is to be heard, it is to be told.

Having an appetite for learning will keep the mind from starving.

No one is indispensable; therefore, it is a good idea to have someone lined up to replace you.

In order to stop digging a hole for yourself, get rid of all your digging devices.

Never take matters into your hands until you have taken them to heart first.

Never give up on what you believe; let your inspiration be your aspiration in order to enhance your motivation.

Your response is sometimes influenced by what you hear, so in a sense, your ears orchestrate your tongue.

The desires of your heart rest at the request of your lips.

There are some things in life you are better without; however, if you lose your heart in the process, you have lost everything.

It is hypocritical to pray for someone you refuse to love.

It is highly impossible to camouflage our ignorance when we refuse to stop talking.

If you are endowed with the gift of speech, you are as valuable as the penmanship of an experienced writer.

The best way to unite people who are feuding is to give them a common enemy.

Anything in your life that you are not willing to give away is not worth purchasing in the first place.

Fear can become a disability if we embrace it.

If you go through life with your head held down, you will obviously miss out on what is ahead.

Learn how to be a good listener before you rush to speak.

You don't have to be a Hummingbird to have a song in your heart, just keep on singing about love.

Think about it: if you are in a league by yourself, who's going to be your competitor?

Those who engage in hate tactics are self-taught "school of love" dropouts.

Words are power; they're supposed to inflate your ego, not deflate it.

One who wants to have his hands in everything must be prepared to get his hands dirty on occasion.

An itching ear is less troublesome than lying lips.

Anything that is half done is not worth half doing.

Don't let your imagination carry you too far from reality unless it is willing to escort you back.

It will be difficult to face tomorrow if you have not achieved your goals today.

A student of the game will make an excellent teaching coach.

The more you learn, the more you will be able to help others.

SECTION 3:
ADVICE TO ENLIGHTEN

Revenge is like a boomerang; it will always come back to you.

All calls to God are toll-free, so why are you waiting for payday to contact Him?

Physiological and emotional stresses are costly; it is important to keep away from those who may find their company entertaining.

Since God has created us in His own image, we have God's DNA.

The measure of everyone's faith is measured by the need.

Don't burn your bridges, especially if you expect to travel the same path day in and day out.

When traveling over a dangerous and unpredictable highway, have a little patience to avoid being a casualty.

You shouldn't override whatever is already functioning properly.

If you continue to play with fire, you should take up another hobby; fire has its advantage, but it has disadvantages as well.

Don't spend an enormous amount of time worrying about what people think of you. What they think is usually not as bad as what they say!

When the Constitution states that all men are created equal, it does not mean equally selfish or equally incompetent.

It's not necessary to tell others what you want to be when you grow up unless you have more growing up to do.

People who don't tend to their own business obviously have too much time on their hands.

You don't want to spend time around untrustworthy people because there are no good benefits you will obtain during the association.

"Been there, done that" does not make you an expert, but it will provide you experience.

Don't take lightly the statement, "What you don't know can't hurt you" because, for example, if you have an undiagnosed illness, it could not only hurt you, it could be fatal.

Don't be so forgetful that you can't find your dignity.

If you are constantly getting burned by a so-called friend, you will be better off if you had just played with fire.

Be careful what comes out of your mouth when you speak to people, because your speech will have the tendency to define you.

Don't allow the volcano of hate to erupt into rivers of haters.

People who have been hurt mentally or physical by someone will eventually hurt others; therefore, hurt people hurt people.

Worrying has no immediate value … it only allows you to rehearse a problem that has not been eliminated or solved.

If you are to have any chance of winning anything, you first have to be in the game.

"Tug-of-war" is played by people trying to pull you toward mischief while you are pulling in the opposite direction.

Some may consider being selfish a positive, denoting strength and independence; however, it is considered by most to be a weakness.

Don't let anyone give you information that they can't back up with supportive data. Likewise, don't permit preachers to give information they can't support with biblical references.

Don't plant anything you aren't prepared to harvest, for if you plant bad words, expressions, and attitudes, you will ultimately reap them.

Courts are designed to settle disputes, not fix stupidity.

Stop judging others unless you have been given a robe and assigned to the bench.

Did you know they are giving away money at jobs? However, you first must be hired.

The person who sings the loudest and has the oddest pitch is usually the one who hasn't had musical training.

Don't be a procrastinator; however, if you are, remember that a delayed decision is still a decision made.

Winning, rather than defeat, is probably a better subject to discuss with a champion.

You can always repeat the truth verbatim, but a lie will continue to change every time you speak.

This is a hint to the selfish: it's not about you as it is about others.

There is no excuse for mistreating those who have mistreated you.

Intelligence and character are the true measure of an educated person.

Don't ask people to follow you if you have no intention of leading them anywhere.

Beware of those who insist on giving answers to questions that have not been asked.

Neighbors are people who not only live next door but who you come in contact with often.

Excuses are delayed failures.

When you try to please everyone, in essence you may not be pleasing anyone.

There are no winners when you play the game of inflicting pain and hatred on others.

We cannot allow ourselves to become a casualty of other people's addictions.

Don't hang on to the people who are holding you back.

The assignment given to you by God will be fulfilled in spite of opposition from your adversaries; expect conflict and trouble throughout the task, but if God is on your side, no one can defeat you.

People who hold you hostage using what they know about your past will not be able to measure up to the forgiveness God has granted you once you repent.

You should recognize that when you point a finger at others' mistakes, your thumb is closer to your face and is pointing back at you.

Beware of busybodies who pretend to give you advice. They aren't sincere in giving you advice and are attempting to get in your business.

Don't hang the phone up on your enemies, but don't hang out with them either.

Don't let the devil control your tongue. He did not create it and is in no position to tell you how to use it.

Unhappy people are more inclined to add up their troubles than count their blessings.

If you are rubbing someone the wrong way, you are obviously too close.

Love is not a communicable disease; however, it should be contagious if it is genuinely expressed.

In order to develop a healthy lifestyle, the word "eliminate" is essential. Eliminate hatred, resentment, jealousy, and grudges.

A foolish man is one who stays up late contemplating how to get even with a person who has wronged him, only to be injured after falling asleep at the wheel en route to the person's residence.

It is odd when a person insists on getting even with another. Vengeance still doesn't belong to us.

Don't select a leader who is afraid to take you where he or she is afraid to go himself or herself.

You may have two targets in view, but you can only hit one at a time, so have patience and approach your goals one at a time.

Everyone should have the highest expectation for himself or herself, but the person you don't have to second guess is Jesus Christ. He's that and more; try Him.

All the days of your life you will not be treated equally, but that shouldn't stop you from giving your all every day of your life.

Don't let your thoughts or motives give character to your conduct.

Reading can save your life; so take time to read the Bible, for it will provide an opportunity for eternal life.

You should not spend time exercising your problems but exercise instead finding solutions.

Keeping company with a wicked person is like allowing an unskilled dancer to take the lead. If he leads long enough, he will take you where you don't want to go.

Pay little attention to those who accuse you falsely and mingle in your business; just don't confuse them with friends while they point their finger.

Doubt is a word that should be stricken from your vocabulary and especially from your mind.

Doubt in God has become the weakness of man.

The person who has caused you to become angry holds a psychological advantage over you.

Don't shatter mirrors in your home just because you don't like the way you see yourself. Change is always one step away.

You can't be a rubber band, but you can learn how to stretch every inch of ability to perform your best.

Just because we think we have an inch of sense doesn't make us a ruler.

It is easier to blame others for the mistakes we created than admit we are the cause.

Having a tattoo does not define you, but your character does.

Remaining silent is not the worst thing to do when you don't know what to say.

In this twenty-first century, it is time for unity to become prominent in our communities. We can accomplish great things by working together.

It is written in our standard language in the holy book that "you will reap what you sow," which can be interpreted as: "Everything you do will come back to you."

Once you realize the Being behind the creation of the "pretty" or "ugly" appearance—as determined by your bias—the outward appearance fades away until it simply no longer matters.

Fear is the first sign of the enemy showing up, in the form of "doubt."

Be careful who you share your vision with because some of your friends will find giants—known as jealousy—in your vision.

Regardless of which occupation you have chosen in life, there are always responsibilities that come with the job.

Your ultimate goal in life is to seek God's justice, whereby He is infinitely righteous in all His dealings with us. God's justice is pictured as two sorts: remuneration, by which He gives reward for goodness, and punitive, by which He deals out punishment.

No matter what you do for a living, the difficulty of that job pales in comparison to the difficulty of another job some of us have in common: being a parent.

Our success or failure is due largely to our attitude.

It is not a violation with the Department of Motor Vehicles to admit that you are intoxicated by the beauty of your spouse even while you are operating a vehicle.

Education is the core and mainstream of all human

activity. If there's an ocean, we'll cross it; if there's a disease, we'll find a cure; if there's a wrong, we'll make it right; if there's a record, we'll break it; and if there's a mountain, we'll reach the top.

You are not considered a child even if you are an adult taking one step at a time.

The problem with some people is that they have just enough conflict in their life to become so miserable that they fail to find the time for problem-solving techniques.

If you are just learning how to swim, never get in over your head. This is good advice regardless of the sport or occupation you are engaged in.

If you get lost during your travel, don't be like the wondering Israelites; for God's sake, ask for directions.

In working with difficult students, the most important thing you should do is be consistent and honest.

Fishing is a good sport for developing patience. The only competition you have is with yourself.

Rejection can be hard to swallow, so you may want to leave it off your menu.

All the answers to every problem you will face in life can be found in the Holy Bible.

It is a good idea to keep your feet clean if you are a

public speaker just in case you slip and put your foot in your mouth.

The best doctors are the ones who cannot bear seeing their patients suffer.

In order to confront a life that deals us constant uncertainties, we must deal ourselves a hand of optimism. We must convince ourselves that the best is yet on the way: a poem has yet to be composed; the best has yet to be sung; the best story has yet to be told; the best painting has yet to be placed on canvas; and the best government has yet to be formed.

Don't spend precious time trying to get even with someone who has wronged you. The Apostle Paul wrote words in Romans 12:17–19 that we must consider when trying to develop strategies for our get-even battle. "Do not repay anyone evil for evil. Be careful to do what is right in the sight of everybody. If it is possible, as it depends on you, live at peace with everyone."

"Disobedient" is a word that you don't want to retain as a novelty.

Should an attitude check be periodically required? If so, would it be difficult finding an examiner without an attitude?

We are all considered servants, but serving without

distinction is not serving at all. We should strive to be a model servant to fulfill our relationship with God.

If you are looking to be restored with trustworthiness, tell the truth no matter what the outcome may be. It will benefit you in the long run. The truth does not need to associate with the lie in order to prevail.

Don't give your past failures an invitation to your coming-out party unless you are willing to face the memories you have been desperately trying to forget.

In order to be a good leader you must know what it is to follow, have good listening skills, accept suggestions, and be a motivator as well as being self-motivating.

There is power in "presence." There are many things you can't do unless you are there in person. One thing that comes to mind is parenting. There is no substitute for being a parent who is on duty and not just on-call.

If you have trouble holding on to things, it is imperative to hold on to the respect you have for yourself and others. If you are a persistent giver of respect, you are due the return of respect. When giving your best, you also learn something about yourself in the process.

"Getting burned" is an expression not only associated with people who play with fire, but with those who have friends who mistreat and or abuse them. Be cautious when dealing with fiery people.

Some people spend a lot of time worrying about what they can't change. Accept the fact that you are not the only person with problems and you will not be the only one who is unable to find a solution. Don't become addicted to worrying about what you can't do, but concentrate on what you can do.

A person with long-term vision will have an impact on generations to come. What a person does not only impacts his life but that of his children's children.

A captain of his ship must know the crewmembers so well that he is able to detect problems by their mannerisms. So it is with the people we work with as well. You may be better off knowing that a person in your company doesn't like you, as opposed to knowing someone who pretends to like you.

Don't waste valuable time calling meetings just to rearrange ignorance. Make sure all meetings are purpose-driven.

Belonging to just any organization is not good enough. We should be associated with organizations that offer superb performance and make a distinctive impact over a long period of time.

Busybodies always have the audacity to get into your business, mainly because they don't have business of their own. When people get into your affairs, don't make them your partner.

The way of birds is by air, the way of boats is by water, the way of serpents is by land, and the way of a thief is by night. Keep your mind sharp so you won't lose your way.

Don't associate with a generation of those who look to do evil toward others. When someone has said an unkind word to you, the most difficult but proper thing to do is to ignore.

A considerate person more often than not thinks before he speaks, but an inconsiderate person blurts out whatever comes to mind. We have to remind ourselves that we are held accountable for whatever we say to others.

A disruptive student may learn from disciplinary action, but a well- behaved student will be most likely benefit from well-thought-out instructions.

It's not a secret that you don't have to reveal your secret to anyone.

You can't be yourself and pretend to be someone else at the same time. My suggestion is to just be yourself, and others will get to know you better.

While traveling through life, don't ignore the warning signs that are designed to make your voyage pleasant and safe.

If you are not a magician, stop playing tricks on people. When you are serious, others will appreciate your maturity.

Going about a right thing the wrong way will not get you to your appointed destination.

Don't be taken aback with things that you disagree with; the time will come when you will be given an opportunity to voice your concerns, and when that times comes, don't be disappointed the second time around.

Fear is a liability, not an asset, so don't bank on it.

Fear can become so selfish that it will consume everyone not bearing its name.

Don't let fear order you around; take charge of yourself.

Animals are branded for the purpose of identification, and humans who are branded with a tattoo are still looking for identification.

Perseverance that is absent from a relationship, a job, or self-improvement will determine how fast the decline will be.

When you are consistently late for appointments, my advice is to leave a day earlier.

Rumors—as opposed to cell phone roamers—have no restricted areas.

People who are magnanimous are generally fulfilled, happy, and satisfied.

Don't hang out with those who have no interest in your success. They will become like nicotine: get you hooked and cause devastation.

The word Passover in the scriptures does not refer to what some people practice in the twenty-first century. Passover does not mean we are to pass over those who need our help.

Dogs dig up bones they have planted, and your enemies dig up dirt on you that they have planted.

"Power" carries around a lot of weight; however, if the weight of power falls on you it could be quite a burden, especially if you are president of the United States.

Unfortunately, people don't use their heads when it comes to preparing for the future. If would be better for some if the future was revealed in advance; however, this would not help those who are poor planners, but it would let them see what they are in for in advance.

When you do evil for evil, there are no good results.

There is nothing wrong with being pragmatic when appropriate, but don't let yourself become arrogant.

You don't have to cater to people just so they will cater

to you; you can go too far going out of your way to satisfy them.

An imposter is a person who does not regard himself worthy of being himself and goes to great length to pretend to be someone else.

It is not necessary to use binoculars to locate phonies; they usually find you.

If you continue to make excuses, eventually you will discover you have a patent on the word.

Use discretion when confronting those who have a scheme to make you wealthy, especially when they see you are doing well all by yourself.

In order to keep your reputation intact, refrain from talking to people who are trying to make friends with your enemies.

The reason words get twisted is because we hear what we want to hear and then add and subtract what we thought we heard. By the time it is repeated, it has been interpreted in our own language.

Being superstitious will cause you to spend more time avoiding the unavoidable.

I'm not aware of what the oldest trick in the world is, but I know Satan has been playing them since the beginning of time.

You don't have to watch your back because you have

volunteers who are doing that for you, and not all for the right reasons.

Words are an extraordinary expression of ideas, yet they can be bitter and cold when spoken with an evil tongue and through deceitful lips.

This is just a warning: be vigilant, stay ahead of the game, and think outside the box. This warning will provide shelter for the storms that will present themselves over the years to come.

SECTION 4:
ADVICE TO INSTRUCT

If you want to be fighter for good and righteous living, let God be your trainer and promoter. He provides all the support you will need to defeat evil.

It is not the force of the drip of water that caused the dent in the cement slab beneath the air conditioner; rather, it was the consistency of the drip that caused the dent. If we are to make a dent in the lives of others, we must be consistent with love for one another.

Don't let the lack of ambition cause you to miss out on the things that are most important to you.

You can't go through it until you get to it. You can't experience what you haven't been exposed to.

Life is too short, so don't spend a long time worrying about nothing; make every moment you live on Earth worth your time.

Be careful how fast you move up; you just might bump into yourself coming back down.

Love does not discriminate, it unifies.

You can fool others by what you say and do, but the reality is that you are only fooling yourself.

Good churchgoers gather with each other rather than scatter one another.

In order to achieve it, your heart must be in it.

If you consider yourself a bad person, remember: something good can come from something bad!

You don't need fireman training to put out fires.

If you are a person who loves to see another person suffer, then you are the person who is sick.

If you want to practice loving others, schedule a session with yourself.

Your body is a temple, and temples are more valuable when they are built up, not torn down. Refrain from doing anything that will damage your health.

Draw the line not with your penmanship but with your character and obedience.

You don't have to be afraid, but it doesn't hurt to be cautious.

If you are serious about losing weight, let me suggest a diet: feed your faith and starve your doubts.

For self-improvement, include laughter in your daily diet.

A good laugh will not only keep the wrinkles away but will keep you upbeat and happy.

Practice doesn't necessarily make you perfect, but it will make you better.

In order to gain favor with God, you have to perform favors for others.

Spirituality looks upon the heart and not the surface of the believer.

The team that performs the best performs together, not as individuals.

God's love for you has no expiration date.

To continue spiritual growth and development, you must overcome those things that have been plaguing you.

Without expecting something in return, do well to as many people as you can. Include in your daily prayers those who don't like you.

When you overcome a deficiency, it should make you realize that real success does not mean giving in but getting over instead.

You can prevent an argument by offering positive comments rather than engaging in negative attacks.

Loving others takes practice, so you should perform this task over and over and over.

Don't magnify your difficulties, maximize your possibilities.

God orders your steps and your stops as well.

Life is like purchasing a suit: very seldom will you find the perfect fit, and alterations become necessary.

Acknowledging that you have made a mistake is not a sign of weakness but of strength.

The saying "treating others as you want to be treated" is not found in Webster's dictionary but in the way we live.

You are not at your best unless you have utilized every ounce of potential in all that you do. If you hold back, you can only blame yourself for your shortcomings.

You can't help it if nature slows down your progress, but there's no excuse if you let a naysayer impede it.

A Bible verse or two a day will help keep the devil away.

Kindness should be like blood flowing through the body—unless it is circulating, it doesn't allow you to be at your best.

You don't need a wristwatch to know that it is time to treat people the way you want to be treated.

Having a good relationship with others is important, but knowing yourself has greater implications.

We know that everything God created was good; therefore, it is necessary that we strive to develop relationships with one another in honor of He who created us.

Don't let your problems make you sick; instead, make your problems sick of you.

Putting your best foot forward has more to do with your heart and head and less to do with your feet.

You can hide your face, but you can't hide your identity.

A good friend is one who will not abandon you when there's a problem and will celebrate with you in your joy.

Don't settle for, "I can if I think I can." Rather, say emphatically, "I can because I know I can."

The promise of love brings about showers of blessings regardless of the season.

A person who looks back while running is obviously afraid of what or who might catch up with him.

We can move forward much quicker if we don't allow our past to hold us back.

A saint can be described as a person who can get along with the worst of people.

One of the most pleasing statements of gratitude in the English language is, "Thank you."

If we could utilize our time being thankful for what we have, be it small or great, we would minimize the time spent complaining about what we don't have.

You don't need to carry a big stick to make your point unless your profession is a hockey player.

If we learn to be slow in judging others, we can learn to be quick in finding good in most.

Don't know what to do when you don't know what to do? Pray. Believe it or not, God has an answer with your name on it just waiting for you to ask.

As a Christian, keeping a low profile is an indication of one who displays humility.

An unexpected source of strength in weakness is repentance.

If you are what you would like to be, it really doesn't matter what others make you out to be. Knowing who you are makes all the difference.

You are never alone, although it sometimes feels that way when you may not have achieved all you would like to accomplish; however, without the Lord, none of what you have done would have been possible. Learn to appreciate what He is doing in your life.

If what you do is in your heart from the beginning, just think how much better your performance would be.

If you were given the opportunity to request anything in the world and it would be granted, what would it be? We must be careful about what we ask for, because if it is granted, we have to live with the decision for the rest of our lives.

Don't be so reluctant to break old habits, especially when those habits have kept you from reaching your potential.

Have you given thought to what God's greater purpose for you is? We rarely know why we are treated the way we are. Perhaps it's to see how strong we are before going through the next test.

Can you make a way out of no way? Probably not, but God can, so let Him be your construction site engineer.

It is recorded in Proverbs 27:17, "As iron sharpens iron, so one man sharpens another." Men who encourage each other will develop better relationships.

When you find joy in what you do, you will do it better. We have a relatively short span on this earth, so it is imperative that we make the best out of our opportunities.

We must strive to keep a sober mind at all times so we can speak with boldness and clarity at any given notice.

Don't be wary of doing well, and don't let the thought of it stop you from doing well.

We must choose our words as carefully as we choose our food. Nothing should enter your mouth unless it provides proper nourishment, and likewise, nothing should come from our mouth unless it is nourishment for the soul.

It doesn't matter how frail your body is or whether you are an advocate of physical fitness. If you devote time to learning, the knowledge you will acquire is mightier than brute strength.

Don't sell yourself out for money or fame, because your reputation is more important.

Don't wait until New Year's celebration to say farewell to the old and ring in the new. Do it as often as a change in your lifestyle dictates.

Talents that have been afforded you should not be kept on ice but used.

To be all you can be may require putting extra time into your preparation.

Never become so satisfied with what you have accomplished that you lose that drive and competitive edge you once had.

Don't forget that your ability is endless.

If we could learn how to intertwine with one another, we could be the rope that pulls others out of their difficulties, rather than the rope used in tug-of-war against one another.

No one likes to be kept waiting, but the Lord is the only person worth waiting for. He doesn't come when we want Him but is there when we need Him the most.

Do not fret if your performance is being assessed, it will benefit you if you are doing well or in need of improvement.

Never allow the hope you have obtained to die; do whatever is necessary to keep hope alive, because so goes hope, so goes you.

If you have developed the habit of telling the truth at all costs, you will attract people who are character-builders.

Never count yourself out during tough times; as long as you have an ounce of strength, keep on fighting.

There's nothing so bad about being a loner; no one arrived with you at birth, and no one will volunteer to leave with you in death.

If the well of prosperity runs dry, don't dig a hole unless you are looking to become prosperous.

You will not be labeled a fortuneteller if you don't give people the impression that you know everything.

When you think about change, think about self-improvement. There is a yearning for being the best you can be.

Figuratively, you may want to break your neck

breaking ties with bad company; the dislocation will do you good.

Exercising your right to vote does nothing for your physique, but it does make you proud, knowing you've made a contribution.

Kindness may not pay, but it pays to be kind.

When you are granted spiritual elevation, it will be necessary to separate yourself from bad habits that will deprive you of any celebration.

You can stop making your haters enemies by making your enemies your friends; love converts.

When those you thought were your friends treat you unfairly, don't give up on everyone; there are still enough sincere people to go around.

Section 5:
Advice to improve Faith

Charles Arthur Shipp, Sr.

Do what you can and let God help with what you're unable to do.

People may pretend to know your past, but only God knows everything about you.

To get to know God is to put into practice what He has given us through His word.

God is omnipresence; therefore, we have comfort in knowing that we are never alone regardless of our circumstances.

The best thing for you is salvation, which is free.

Prayer is an energy that is capable of soaring above the clouds into the cosmos.

Christianity is a role you don't have to audition for.

If you want to maintain your peace of mind, develop more faith in what you do to please God.

A person who has reached a peak in his life is capable of climbing back up once he has fallen down.

Faith is giving God the praise in advance for what you expect will happen.

Knowledge is believing that you know what you know beyond a shadow of a doubt.

Without going through tests, you won't have a testimony.

Goodness can provide a harvest even in the midst of a drought.

This is not a good time to complain about what someone is trying to do to you, but rather concentrate on what God is doing for you.

In order for your faith to be increased, you must use what you have already been given, which is a close association with Christ.

Faith is an awesome companion to take with you on your life's journey.

Faith is believing that something can resolve from nothing.

Careless words always have a way of finding you out.

What's in the heart will eventually come out through the mouth.

Courage is defined as the ability to walk away from the familiar to face the unfamiliar.

When you do something wrong, you should be more concerned with the person you can't see as opposed to the one you can.

In Philippians 4:13, the Apostle Paul stated, "I can do all things through Christ who strengthens me." Through faith, we can do those things that seem impossible to us as human beings.

A guide is a person who has been hired to keep you from getting lost, but he is ineffective if you take the lead while not knowing where you are going.

There is strength in believing.

How well you perceive an idea will determine the outcome.

Whatever is done behind closed doors is not necessarily done in closed session. God sees all that we do and hears all that is said.

If you find yourself struggling with problems that are keeping you awake at night, turn them over to Jesus. He's up all night anyway.

Love is like Novocain: give it time and it will work.

While hating others, you are infecting yourself with a bacteria called sin, and the only cure is repentance.

While traveling through the journey of life, you may use an atlas, a compass, or even a GPS; however, if you don't have Jesus, you will still get lost.

You will never get lost if you travel with Christ.

Like the prodigal son, the real change occurs with a person when he or she comes to himself or herself.

There are blessings in seeking the things that are spiritual; therefore, press toward the mark for the prize of the higher calling in Christ Jesus.

Honest children are more likely to trust others.

Don't put your faith in man's wisdom but in God's power.

If you are looking to find your way to God, keep the faith. He will send escorts know as grace and mercy.

The essence of genius is to know who to put your trust and faith in.

Whatever your problems are in life, you don't have to face them alone.

Never doubt the outcome when asking for God's guidance.

Trust the Lord even when there are difficulties in your life.

Your faith should not be grounded in material things but in the things from above.

Don't let fear keep you from climbing the ladder of success. God has not given us the spirit of fear, so press on.

Humbleness has its benefits, for God is merciful unto the humble.

Nothing is asked to be given by you in faith that has not been given first by God. He has given willingly, ungrudgingly, and unselfishly to us all.

Believing is about doing; however, you first must believe before you can see results.

Be strong in the Lord, for He is able to give you abundant strength.

Perseverance is not looking back at what you have done but ahead to what is expected to be done in the future.

What a person believes is what he will end up being.

If you want to make your life journey easier, stop carrying around your burdens.

You don't have to worry about where you step if you are walking with the King.

A relationship is not merely based on having a common interest but on faith you have developed in each other throughout the relationship.

Hold on to your faith and never let go, for it will enable you to overcome cruelty and injustice thrown your way.

Once you have completed a difficult task, the award is much greater than the work that was done.

Whatever predicament you find yourself in, God can lead you out.

It is great being in the land of the living, but we

must ask ourselves, "What am I living for if not for God?"

There are medications prescribed for cleaning out the body's systems, but confession is the only thing that will cleanse the soul.

Always reserve enough energy to be strong enough to say "I'm sorry."

The only thing breakable in a man-made church is the commandments.

A person without hope is just as bad as the person trying to fill a bucket with a hole in it.

You don't have to prove to others what you have proven to yourself, especially if you are satisfied with the results.

It is advisable to exercise the body regularly to maintain good health, but it is equally important to exercise your faith by placing your trust in a greater power, especially when things are not going the way you think they should.

Build your lifestyle with a firm foundation, so when the storm of disappointments and chaos troubles you, you will be unshaken.

Those who trust in God are given increased strength, even when they have no might.

Don't be discouraged by the declining economy and

the letdowns we are experiencing; just don't throw in the towel. Have faith that things will get better.

A vision without a task creates a visionary; work without a vision is drudgery; and a vision with work makes a missionary.

If you feel uncertain about the task you have been assigned, don't try to do it alone; put it in the hands of God, and you can rest assured that it will get done.

Once we realize that we are not really the owner of what we possess, we will put less emphasis on ownership and more focus on the lender.

You don't have to always know how you got what you have; it is by God's grace that He knows what we need, and He has the power to award us without us asking.

The way of the Lord is known to everyone, but you have to seek Him yourself.

Weakness is the result of loss of power. When you see that you are becoming negative, hook up with someone positive to restart your life.

Your enemy enslaves you while God empowers you.

If you can see what others can't, you can have what others don't have.

God uses foolish things to get the attention of the wise.

It is wise to have good friends or companions, for if one should fall, another is there to pick you up.

The family circle has no ending; we are all brothers and sisters in Christ Jesus.

Whatever you do, never give up; find inspiration to your aspiration and it will give you motivation.

Have faith enough to know that God can do what is considered impossible.

We learn by association. If we associate with faithless people, we learn lessons that will diminish our faith.

For reassurance, keep a mustard seed of faith wherever you go.

If you have the courage to stand in the midst of turmoil, you will not fall for the least surge of disappointment.

Never permit doubt to prevent you from reaching those future goals you have set for yourself.

When you are down to your last dime, when it seems like all hope is gone and friends have abandoned you, keep enough faith to remember "ASAP": Always Stop and Pray.

Faith will allow you to perform self-examinations to determine what spiritual deficiencies you may have and the willingness to overcome them.

When taking a faith test, you must be willing to surrender those things that are holding you hostage and keeping you from doing what is right.

SECTION 6:
ADVICE FOR INSPIRATION

Having access to the whole armor of God is a uniform that is not purchased with gold or silver but is provided to all who want to be equipped to serve the Lord.

Pressure presents itself when you have to make quick and important decisions; therefore, it is advisable to stay as calm as possible and make the decision you can live with.

You may not have the voice of an angel, but you can express the attitude of angels by showing your love for others.

While the president has secret servicemen to protect him, we are protected by heavenly angels.

Each one of us can be a student of each other's genius.

Having problems are not always as bad as you think; problems sometimes exist to keep one from being conceited.

When someone hurts you, you need to seek help, not revenge.

Love is the real champion in every competition.

Love never fails us; we fail to love.

Love will work when you work it!

Don't leave home without taking love with you

because it is the only weapon that is powerful enough to defeat evil.

Understanding God's plan for you will help you preserve in fulfilling your Christian responsibilities, regardless of whom or what tries to prevent you from achieving His desires for you.

Words are powerful; they are best utilized when they build you up, not destroy your character.

Don't sit at the table of hallucination and hypocrisy if you expect to receive spiritual nourishment for the soul.

Regardless of what you see, God sees the best in me.

Overcome pessimistic notions by surrounding yourself with an optimistic outlook on life.

We should never boast when we give to the unfortunate, for it is not the people we give to but God.

Make every positive adventure you engage in more than just an event, and it will become your lifestyle.

A person's stamina is not determined merely by how many times he has been knocked down but how many times he is able get back on his feet.

You have been wonderfully made, so consider yourself as being customized by the best.

You already have the ability to be whatever you want to be, but your goals will not be realized without hard work and strong determination.

In order to be successful in life, you have to have a vision, set priorities, and be faithful in all that you do.

Since most of our hurt comes through relationships, so will the healing.

You can strive to be both holy and whole. Make God the head of your life, and He will provide you with the necessities to fulfill the desires of your heart according to His will.

It is gratifying when you help someone who is less fortunate than yourself. As a matter of fact, that is why we are blessed in the first place. Keep blessing and you will be blessed.

You don't have to be perfect in what you do, but if you give what you do your best, you are considered a winner!

Find a way to control your anger. Most of the poor decisions that are made are the results of one losing the ability to stay calm under difficult circumstances.

An important lesson to be learned in life is to practice being patient. Don't be anxious for everything because if it is meant to be, it will.

When life becomes dreary, you need to find an anchor that will keep you from drifting into the deep waters of despair.

To hang out with people of high intelligence is, in a sense, an opportunity to drink from their inspirational wellspring, or at least be directed to sources that might satisfy our intellectual thirst.

A stalwart leader has his feet planted firmly in the soil of his followers' hopes and aspirations.

Make sure the road you have chosen will get you to your destination. On the other hand, be willing to change if you realize you are headed in the wrong direction.

Show gratitude for what you have received by taking good care of what you have been given.

A good attitude is a prescription for prosperity.

One of the many reasons we should be proud to live in America is that we don't have to get permission to be all that we can be.

Compassion begins on the inside, and like a volcano, it erupts on the outside with a flare of caring, sharing, and humility.

You don't have to have eloquence of speech to communicate with God. He understands before you speak because He knows your thoughts.

When you have made inappropriate remarks toward another, don't add to your problem by refusing to admit that you are wrong. The sooner you acknowledge your guilt, the quicker you can put the wrong behind you and move on with your life.

In an attempt to avenge someone who has wronged you, think of all the goodness you have been granted, and you will realize that your animosity is insignificant after all.

It is natural for one to be anxious occasionally; however, we are reminded that while we wait, our strength is being renewed so we can endure to the end.

Like the moon that hovers over and watches the exuberant lake, and like the birds that keep harmony with the wind whistling through the forest on a clear day, our souls are guided by their creator.

Take a little time to give thanks; it is the least you can do to show an appreciation for life itself and what God is doing in your life.

God is so spectacular that we have not seen Him at His best, but if you continue in His word, He will show you the rest.

God wants us to be successful and/or prosperous in whatever we do, so don't be afraid to put your trust in Him.

There's a game that children play called "Hide and Seek." The purpose of the game is to hide from the leader, so as to be the last player to be found by the leader. Today, Jesus is not hiding from us; rather He invites us to seek Him while we're still in the game of life.

There is a good reason we try to do things well, and that is because of the need to be great. Also, it brings about an understanding and an appreciation of who and whose we are.

Don't be surprised by your ability to perform at a high level. You are a product of God's great creation. Everything He made was good, and since man and woman were made last, He saved the best for last.

You are familiar with the statement, "Sticks and stones may break my bones, but words will never harm me." Let me set the record straight: words have the power to penetrate where no sword can touch, for good or for evil. So a good practice is to use your tongue constructively.

Be a Good Samaritan and help those who have fallen on hard times. If you are merciful unto the least, the lost, and the left out, mercy will look out for you.

Occasionally, you have to stoop low (way down) in order to pull yourself up by your own bootstraps.

Take good care of whatever craft you have been blessed with and eventually it'll take care of you.

Never think of yourself more highly than you are; rather, you must recognize your limitations and conduct yourself accordingly.

Life is similar to a marathon, and some runners will finish before others; however, the distinct difference is that everyone is guaranteed to finish. The race is not given to the swift but to the person who endures to the finish.

Don't commit yourself to quitting when faced with adversities, but commit yourself to finding a solution; it will occupy your mind with positive thoughts.

If it's not broken, break it! In other words, stop doing what you have always done if it gets you the same bad results.

It is impossible to wear out your welcome if you are in the house of the Lord; the longer you stay, the more you are made welcome.

Don't be frightened by the word "change." Change is necessary in order to arrive at the results you need. Remember, change is not only good when things are going wrong but also when things are going right.

A good teacher does not limit himself to just teaching but to learning as well. If you aren't learning from the students you teach, don't be disappointed if they aren't learning from you.

It is better that we learn how to share with one another. Receiving information is a privilege, not a right, but sharing information is the right thing to do.

People can easily see what you are wearing on the outside, but let them see what you are wearing on the inside by exhibiting a good heart.

For better or for worse, for richer or poorer, until death do us part, we should love the Lord with all our heart, mind, and soul.

There can't be promotion without "motion."

Follow your heart, and if things do not go according to plan, at least you will know who got you lost.

When you hit rock bottom, land on your feet so you will be in position to spring back up again.

About The Author

Charles Arthur Shipp, Sr. was born in Washington DC. He graduated from Johnson C. Smith University, Charlotte, North Carolina, with a bachelor's degree in elementary education, from Virginia, Commonwealth University, Richmond, Virginia with a master's degree in Elementary Education, and a postgraduate degree in public school administration. He retired after forty-two years as a teacher, coach, and principal. His last ten years were spent as principal of John G. Wood Alternative School in Richmond, Virginia, where he had a 100 percent graduation rate. He resides in Richmond, Virginia.